Homemade Treats

For

Your Dog

70+ snack recipes for your furry friend

Grace Mathew

TABLE OF CONTENT

INTRODUCTION

Hello there! I'm thrilled to welcome you to the world of homemade dog treats through the pages of this cookbook. My name is Grace, and I'm not just a dog lover; I'm a passionate advocate for treating our furry companions to the very best.

For as long as I can remember, I've shared a special bond with dogs. They've been my faithful companions through thick and thin, offering unwavering love and loyalty. In return, I've always strived to provide them with the healthiest and most delicious treats possible. Over the years, I've experimented, perfected, and collected an array of homemade dog treat recipes that have brought joy and tail-wagging delight to my four-legged friends.

This cookbook is a labor of love, born from a desire to share my knowledge and passion with fellow dog enthusiasts like you. Whether you're a seasoned baker or a kitchen novice, you'll find recipes here that are easy to follow, using wholesome ingredients that ensure your furry friends receive the nutrition and flavor they deserve.

As you flip through these pages, you'll discover treats for every occasion, from simple everyday rewards to special celebration goodies. Each recipe is crafted with love and care, and I hope that baking these treats for your beloved dogs will bring as much joy to your heart as it has to mine.

So, grab your apron, preheat that oven, and let's embark on a delightful journey of baking and bonding with your four-legged companions. Together, we'll create tail-wagging moments and cherished memories that will last a lifetime. Thank you for joining me on this delicious adventure!

CONVERSIONS CHARTS

You can utilise these charts to quickly convert metric measurements to standard/imperial measurements

Oven Temperature Conversion

Standard	Metric
1/5 tsp	1 ml
1 tsp	5 ml
1 tbsp	15ml
1 fl.oz	30 ml
1 c	237 ml
1pt	473 ml
1 qt	.95 l

CELSIUS (DEGREES)	FAHRENHEIT
120C	250F
160C	320F
180C	350F
205C	400F
220C	425F

US to Metric Cooking Conversions

1 gal **Metric**	3.8 l **Standard**	
1 qt	1 qt	**Liquid Measurements (Volume)**
500 g	3.854 g	
500 g	17 tbspz	**Dry Measurements (Weight)**
240 ml	35 (& fl.oz)	
1 litre	34 fl.oz	

THINGS TO NOTE:

1. Safety First: it is important to use pet-safe ingredients and avoiding harmful substances like chocolate, onions, and garlic.

2. Ingredient Quality: the use of high-quality, fresh ingredients for the best results in homemade treats is advisable.

3. Portion Control: make sure there is guidance on appropriate treat sizes to prevent overfeeding and maintain a healthy weight for dogs.

4. Allergen Alerts: make sure you know what ingredients your dogs are allergic to.

Remember to cool the treats completely before giving them to your furry friend and store any leftovers in an airtight container. Enjoy making these tasty homemade treats for your dog!

REMEMBER TO ALWAYS CHECK WITH YOUR VETERINARIAN BEFORE INTRODUCING NEW TREATS INTO YOUR DOG'S DIET, ESPECIALLY IF THEY HAVE ANY DIETARY RESTRICTIONS OR ALLERGIES.

BAKED TREATS

1. Peanut Butter Banana Bites

Ingredients:

- 1 ripe banana

- 1/2 cup natural peanut butter

- 1 cup whole wheat flour

Process:

1. Preheat your oven to 350°F (175°C).

2. Mash the banana and mix it with peanut butter in a bowl.

3. Gradually add the whole wheat flour and stir until you have a dough.

4. Roll out the dough and cut it into bite-sized pieces or use cookie cutters.

5. Place them on a baking sheet and bake for 10-15 minutes or until golden brown. Let them cool before serving.

2.. Pumpkin and Oat Biscuits

Ingredients:

- 1 cup canned pumpkin

- 2 cups oats

- 1/4 cup water

Process:

1. Preheat your oven to 350°F (175°C).

2. Combine pumpkin and oats in a bowl.

3. Add water and mix until a dough forms.

4. Roll out the dough and cut into shapes or use a cookie cutter.

5. Place on a baking sheet and bake for 20-25 minutes or until firm and dry.

3. Sweet Potato Chews

Ingredients:

- 2 sweet potatoes

Process:

1. Preheat your oven to 250°F (120°C).

2. Slice sweet potatoes into thin rounds.

3. Place them on a baking sheet and bake for 2-3 hours until they become chewy.

4. Chicken and Cheese Dog Treats

Ingredients:

- 1 cup cooked chicken, shredded

- 1 cup shredded cheddar cheese

- 1 cup whole wheat flour

Process:

1. Preheat your oven to 350°F (175°C).

2. Combine chicken, cheese, and flour in a bowl.

3. Knead into a dough and roll it out.

4. Cut into desired shapes and bake for 15-20 minutes until golden brown.

5. Apple and Carrot Pupcakes

Ingredients:

- 1 apple, grated

- 1 carrot, grated

- 1 cup whole wheat flour

- 1 egg

- 1/4 cup water

Process:

1. Preheat your oven to 350°F (175°C).

2. Mix grated apple, grated carrot, flour, egg, and water in a bowl.

3. Pour the batter into muffin tins.

4. Bake for 20-25 minutes or until a toothpick comes out clean.

6. Blueberry and Oat Cookies

Ingredients:

- 1 cup rolled oats

- 1/2 cup blueberries

- 1 ripe banana

Process:

1. Preheat your oven to 350°F (175°C).

2. Mash the banana and mix with oats and blueberries.

3. Drop spoonfuls onto a baking sheet.

4. Bake for 12-15 minutes until firm.

7. Salmon and Sweet Potato Bites

Ingredients:

- 1 cup canned salmon, drained

- 1 cup mashed sweet potato

- 1 egg

- 2 cups whole wheat flour

Process:

1. Preheat your oven to 350°F (175°C).

2. Mix salmon, sweet potato, egg, and flour until a dough forms.

3. Roll out and cut into bite-sized pieces.

4. Bake for 20-25 minutes until crispy.

8. Cheese and Bacon Twists

Ingredients:

- 1 cup shredded cheddar cheese

- 1/4 cup cooked bacon bits

- 1 cup whole wheat flour

- 1/2 cup water

Process:

1. Preheat your oven to 350°F (175°C).

2. Mix cheese, bacon, flour, and water to form a dough.

3. Roll into ropes and twist them.

4. Bake for 15-20 minutes or until golden brown.

9. Spinach and Cheese Bites

Ingredients:

- 1/2 cup chopped spinach

- 1 cup shredded mozzarella cheese

- 1 cup whole wheat flour

- 1/4 cup water

Process:

1. Preheat your oven to 350°F (175°C).

2. Combine spinach, cheese, flour, and water in a bowl.

3. Shape into bite-sized pieces and bake for 15-20 minutes until crispy.

10. Turkey and Cranberry Treats

Ingredients:

- 1 cup cooked turkey, finely chopped

- 1/4 cup dried cranberries

- 1 cup brown rice flour

- 1/4 cup chicken broth

Process:

1. Preheat your oven to 350°F (175°C).

2. Mix turkey, cranberries, flour, and chicken broth into a dough.

3. Roll out and cut into shapes.

4. Bake for 15-20 minutes until firm.

11. Carrot and Parsley Dog Biscuits

Ingredients:

- 2 cups oat flour

- 1/2 cup grated carrots

- 2 tablespoons fresh parsley, chopped

- 1/4 cup water

Process:

1. Preheat your oven to 350°F (175°C).

2. Combine oat flour, grated carrots, and chopped parsley in a bowl.

3. Add water and mix until a dough forms.

4. Roll out the dough and cut into biscuits.

5. Place on a baking sheet and bake for 20-25 minutes or until they are crispy.

12. Pumpkin and Peanut Butter Pupcakes

Ingredients:

- 1 cup canned pumpkin

- 1/4 cup peanut butter

- 1 1/2 cups whole wheat flour

- 1 egg

Process:

1. Preheat your oven to 350°F (175°C).

2. Mix pumpkin, peanut butter, flour, and egg in a bowl.

3. Pour the batter into cupcake liners.

4. Bake for 20-25 minutes or until a toothpick comes out clean.

13. Tuna and Cheddar Catfish Crackers

Ingredients:

- 1 can of tuna in water, drained

- 1 cup cheddar cheese, shredded

- 1 cup oat flour

Process:

1. Preheat your oven to 350°F (175°C).

2. Blend tuna and cheddar cheese in a food processor until smooth.

3. Add oat flour and blend until a dough forms.

4. Roll out the dough and cut into fish shapes.

5. Place on a baking sheet and bake for 10-15 minutes or until they turn golden brown.

14. Chicken and Rice Dog Donuts

Ingredients:

- 1 cup cooked chicken, shredded

- 1 cup cooked rice

- 1/4 cup chicken broth

- 1/4 cup oat flour

Process:

1. Preheat your oven to 350°F (175°C).

2. Mix shredded chicken, cooked rice, chicken broth, and oat flour in a bowl.

3. Form the mixture into donut shapes.

4. Place on a baking sheet and bake for 20-25 minutes until firm.

15. Blueberry and Banana Frozen Treats

Ingredients:

- 1 ripe banana

- 1/2 cup blueberries

- 1/2 cup plain yogurt

Process:

1. Blend banana, blueberries, and yogurt until smooth.

2. Pour the mixture into silicone molds or ice cube trays.

3. Freeze until solid and serve as a cool treat.

16. Apple and Cinnamon Popsicles

Ingredients:

- 1 apple, grated

- A pinch of cinnamon

- 1 cup plain yogurt

- A splash of water

Process:

1. Mix grated apple, cinnamon, yogurt, and a splash of water.

2. Pour the mixture into popsicle molds.

3. Freeze until solid and serve as a refreshing treat.

17. Turkey and Veggie Meatballs

Ingredients:

- 1 cup ground turkey

- 1/2 cup grated zucchini

- 1/2 cup grated carrot

- 1/2 cup rolled oats

Process:

1. Preheat your oven to 350°F (175°C).

2. Mix ground turkey, grated zucchini, grated carrot, and rolled oats.

3. Form the mixture into meatballs.

4. Place on a baking sheet and bake for 15-20 minutes until cooked through.

18. Salmon and Spinach Balls

Ingredients:

- 1 can of salmon, drained and flaked

- 1/2 cup steamed spinach, chopped

- 1 egg

- 1/2 cup oat flour

Process:

1. Preheat your oven to 350°F (175°C).

2. Combine salmon, chopped spinach, egg, and oat flour.

3. Form the mixture into balls.

4. Place on a baking sheet and bake for 15-20 minutes until firm.

19. Beef and Cheese Twists

Ingredients:

- 1 cup lean ground beef, cooked and drained

- 1 cup shredded cheddar cheese

- 1 cup whole wheat flour

- A splash of water

Process:

1. Preheat your oven to 350°F (175°C).

2. Mix cooked beef, cheddar cheese, whole wheat flour, and a splash of water.

3. Roll into ropes and twist them.

4. Bake for 15-20 minutes or until golden brown.

20. Peanut Butter and Jelly Treats

Ingredients:

- 1/2 cup natural peanut butter

- 1/4 cup unsweetened applesauce

- 1 cup whole wheat flour

- 1/4 cup dried cranberries (for "jelly")

Process:

1. Preheat your oven to 350°F (175°C).

2. Combine peanut butter, applesauce, and flour in a bowl.

3. Roll out the dough and cut into shapes.

4. Place a dried cranberry in the center of each treat.

5. Bake for 15-20 minutes until firm.

NON BAKED TREATS

1. Frozen Banana Bites

Ingredients:

- 2 ripe bananas

- 1/2 cup plain yogurt

- 1/4 cup peanut butter

Process:

1. Slice the bananas into rounds.

2. Mix yogurt and peanut butter until smooth.

3. Dip banana slices into the yogurt mixture.

4. Place them on a baking sheet lined with parchment paper.

5. Freeze until solid and serve as frozen treats.

2. No-Bake Peanut Butter Balls

Ingredients:

- 1 cup rolled oats

- 1/2 cup natural peanut butter

- 1/4 cup honey

Process:

1. Mix rolled oats, peanut butter, and honey in a bowl.

2. Roll the mixture into bite-sized balls.

3. Place them on a baking sheet lined with parchment paper.

4. Refrigerate until firm and serve.

3. Watermelon Popsicles

Ingredients:

- Fresh watermelon, seedless

Process:

1. Cut watermelon into small cubes or use a melon baller.

2. Insert a dog-friendly popsicle stick into each piece.

3. Freeze until solid and serve as a refreshing treat.

4. Frozen Pumpkin and Yogurt Treats

Ingredients:

- 1/2 cup canned pumpkin

- 1/2 cup plain yogurt

Process:

1. Mix canned pumpkin and yogurt until smooth.

2. Spoon the mixture into silicone molds or ice cube trays.

3. Freeze until solid and serve as cool treats.

5. Apple Crunch Popsicles

Ingredients:

- 1 apple, grated

- 1 cup plain yogurt

Process:

1. Mix grated apple and yogurt.

2. Pour the mixture into popsicle molds.

3. Freeze until solid and serve as a crunchy, icy treat.

6. Carrot and Peanut Butter Bones

Ingredients:

- 2 large carrots

- 1/4 cup natural peanut butter

Process:

1. Slice carrots into thick rounds.

2. Spread peanut butter on one side of each carrot round.

3. Press two rounds together to create "bone" shapes.

4. Freeze until firm and serve.

7. Blueberry and Cottage Cheese Drops

Ingredients:

- 1 cup blueberries

- 1/2 cup low-fat cottage cheese

Process:

1. Blend blueberries and cottage cheese until smooth.

2. Drop spoonfuls onto a baking sheet lined with parchment paper.

3. Freeze until solid and serve as small, fruity bites.

8. Cranberry and Turkey Delights

Ingredients:

- 1/2 cup cooked turkey, finely chopped

- 1/4 cup dried cranberries

- 1/4 cup rolled oats

Process:

1. Mix chopped turkey, dried cranberries, and rolled oats.

2. Form into small, bite-sized treats.

3. Refrigerate until firm and serve.

9. Spinach and Cheese Stuffed Kongs

Ingredients:

- Kong dog toy

- Cooked spinach, chopped

- Low-fat cottage cheese

Process:

1. Fill a Kong toy with a mixture of chopped cooked spinach and low-fat cottage cheese.

2. Freeze until solid and give it to your dog as a stuffed, interactive treat.

10. Frozen Berry Bliss

Ingredients:

- 1/2 cup mixed berries (blueberries, strawberries, raspberries)

- 1/2 cup plain yogurt

Process:

1. Mash the mixed berries or blend them into a puree.

2. Mix the berry puree with plain yogurt.

3. Pour the mixture into ice cube trays or silicone molds.

4. Freeze until solid and serve as fruity, frozen treats.

11. Cheese and Apple Stacks

Ingredients:

- Slices of apple

- Low-fat cheese slices

Process:

1. Cut apple slices and low-fat cheese into small pieces.

2. Alternate stacking apple and cheese pieces.

3. Serve as a tasty, crunchy snack.

12. Pumpkin and Carrot Popsicles

Ingredients:

- 1/2 cup canned pumpkin

- 1/2 cup grated carrots

- A splash of water

Process:

1. Mix canned pumpkin, grated carrots, and a splash of water.

2. Pour the mixture into popsicle molds.

3. Freeze until solid and offer as cool, veggie-packed popsicles.

13. Frozen Green Bean Crunchers

Ingredients:

- Cooked and cooled green beans

Process:

1. Steam or blanch green beans until tender and cool.

2. Freeze them and serve as a healthy, crunchy snack.

14. Apple and Peanut Butter Slices

Ingredients:

- Slices of apple

- Natural peanut butter

Process:

1. Spread a thin layer of peanut butter on apple slices.

2. Serve as a delicious and nutritious treat.

15. Yummy Yogurt Drops

Ingredients:

- Plain yogurt

Process:

1. Drop spoonfuls of plain yogurt onto a baking sheet lined with parchment paper.

2. Freeze until solid and serve as small, creamy bites.

16. Coconut and Banana Bites

Ingredients:

- Unsweetened coconut flakes

- Slices of banana

Process:

1. Dip banana slices into unsweetened coconut flakes.

2. Serve as a tropical-flavored, crunchy treat.

17. Melon Medley Chunks

Ingredients:

- Chunks of melon (e.g., cantaloupe, honeydew)

Process:

1. Cut melon into small, bite-sized chunks.

2. Offer as a refreshing, hydrating treat.

18. Tuna and Green Pea Popsicles

Ingredients:

- 1 can of tuna in water, drained

- Cooked and cooled green peas

Process:

1. Blend tuna and green peas into a mixture.

2. Pour the mixture into popsicle molds.

3. Freeze until solid and serve as a savory popsicle.

19. Peanut Butter and Banana Stuffed Kong

Ingredients:

- Kong dog toy

- Natural peanut butter

- Slices of banana

Process:

1. Fill a Kong toy with slices of banana and a dollop of peanut butter.

2. Seal the ends with more peanut butter.

3. Give it to your dog for a challenging, tasty treat.

20. Spinach and Blueberry Frozen Cubes

Ingredients:

- Handful of fresh spinach leaves

- Handful of fresh blueberries

- Water

Process:

1. Blend spinach, blueberries, and a little water until smooth.

2. Pour the mixture into ice cube trays.

3. Freeze until solid and serve as a nutritious and cooling snack.

21. Frozen Carrot Popsicles

Ingredients:

- Baby carrots

Process:

1. Simply place baby carrots in the freezer.

2. Freeze until they are icy and serve as a cooling and crunchy treat.

These non-baked treats are easy to prepare and provide a variety of flavors and textures for your dog to enjoy. Have fun making these homemade goodies for your furry companion!

MEAT FREE TREATS

1. Peanut Butter and Banana Frozen Bites

Ingredients:

- 1 ripe banana

- 1/2 cup natural peanut butter

- 1/4 cup plain yogurt

Process:

1. Mash the ripe banana.

2. Mix mashed banana, peanut butter, and yogurt until smooth.

3. Spoon the mixture into silicone molds or ice cube trays.

4. Freeze until solid and serve as a cool and creamy treat.

2. Coconut and Banana Bites

Ingredients:

- 1 ripe banana

- 1/4 cup unsweetened shredded coconut

- 1/4 cup rolled oats

Process:

1. Mash the ripe banana.

2. Mix mashed banana, shredded coconut, and rolled oats until combined.

3. Form small bite-sized balls from the mixture.

4. Refrigerate until they are firm and serve.

3. Sweet Potato and Peanut Butter Popsicles

Ingredients:

- 1 sweet potato, cooked and mashed

- 1/2 cup natural peanut butter

- A splash of water

Process:

1. Mix mashed sweet potato, natural peanut butter, and a splash of water until smooth.

2. Pour the mixture into popsicle molds.

3. Freeze until solid and serve as a frozen, tasty treat.

4. Banana and Peanut Butter Pupsicles

Ingredients:

- 2 ripe bananas

- 1/2 cup natural peanut butter

- 1/2 cup plain yogurt

Process:

1. Mash the ripe bananas.

2. Mix mashed bananas, peanut butter, and yogurt until smooth.

3. Pour the mixture into silicone molds or ice cube trays.

4. Freeze until solid and serve as frozen treats.

5. Sweet Potato and Carrot treats

Ingredients:

- 1 sweet potato

- 2 carrots

Process:

1. Peel and slice the sweet potato and carrots into thin rounds.

2. Place them on a baking sheet lined with parchment paper.

3. Dehydrate or air-dry them until they become chewy.

6. Blueberry and Oat Energy Bites

Ingredients:

- 1 cup rolled oats

- 1/2 cup fresh blueberries

- 1/4 cup unsweetened applesauce

Process:

1. Blend rolled oats and fresh blueberries until combined.

2. Mix the blended mixture with unsweetened applesauce.

3. Roll into bite-sized balls and refrigerate until firm.

7. Apple and Cheddar Stuffed Kongs

Ingredients:

- Kong dog toy

- Slices of apple

- Small cubes of cheddar cheese

Process:

1. Fill a Kong toy with slices of apple and cubes of cheddar cheese.

2. Seal the ends with a bit of peanut butter.

3. Give it to your dog for a challenging, interactive treat.

8. Spinach and Cheese Poppers

Ingredients:

- 1/2 cup chopped spinach

- 1 cup shredded cheddar cheese

- 1/2 cup plain yogurt

Process:

1. Mix chopped spinach, shredded cheddar cheese, and plain yogurt in a bowl.

2. Drop spoonfuls onto a baking sheet lined with parchment paper.

3. Freeze until solid and serve as bite-sized, creamy snacks.

9. Carrot and Zucchini Bites

Ingredients:

- 1 carrot

- 1 zucchini

- 1/4 cup vegetable broth

Process:

1. Grate the carrot and zucchini.

2. Mix the grated vegetables with vegetable broth.

3. Shape into small bite-sized treats and refrigerate until firm.

10. Pumpkin and Cinnamon Stars

Ingredients:

- 1 cup canned pumpkin

- 1/2 teaspoon ground cinnamon

- 1 1/2 cups oat flour

Process:

1. Mix canned pumpkin, ground cinnamon, and oat flour in a bowl.

2. Roll out the dough and cut into star shapes.

3. Refrigerate until they become firm and serve.

11. Broccoli and Cheese Bites

Ingredients:

- 1 cup steamed and chopped broccoli

- 1 cup shredded mozzarella cheese

- 1/4 cup unsweetened applesauce

Process:

1. Combine steamed and chopped broccoli, shredded mozzarella cheese, and unsweetened applesauce.

2. Roll into small balls and refrigerate until firm.

12. Pumpkin and Cranberry Drops

Ingredients:

- 1/2 cup canned pumpkin

- 1/4 cup dried cranberries

- 1/2 cup rolled oats

Process:

1. Mix canned pumpkin, dried cranberries, and rolled oats until combined.

2. Drop spoonfuls onto a baking sheet.

3. Refrigerate until they become firm and serve as small, flavorful bites.

13. Watermelon Cubes

Ingredients:

- Fresh watermelon, seedless

Process:

1. Cut seedless watermelon into small cubes.

2. Offer as a hydrating and refreshing treat.

14. Peanut Butter and Banana Roll-Ups

Ingredients:

- Whole wheat tortillas

- Natural peanut butter

- Bananas, sliced

Process:

1. Spread a thin layer of peanut butter on a whole wheat tortilla.

2. Place banana slices evenly over the peanut butter.

3. Roll up the tortilla and slice it into bite-sized pieces.

15. Celery and Peanut Butter Ants on a Log

Ingredients:

- Celery sticks

- Natural peanut butter

- Raisins

Process:

1. Spread peanut butter onto celery sticks.

2. Place raisins on top of the peanut butter to resemble "ants on a log."

16. Coconut and Chia Seed Pudding

Ingredients:

- 1 cup unsweetened coconut milk

- 2 tablespoons chia seeds

- 1/2 teaspoon honey (optional)

Process:

1. Mix coconut milk, chia seeds, and honey (if using) in a bowl.

2. Refrigerate for a few hours or overnight until it thickens into a pudding-like consistency.

3. Serve small amounts as a nutritious dessert.

17. Spinach and Apple Smoothie Cubes

Ingredients:

- Handful of fresh spinach leaves

- 1 apple, cored and chopped

- Water

Process:

1. Blend fresh spinach leaves, chopped apple, and a little water until smooth.

2. Pour the mixture into ice cube trays.

3. Freeze until solid and offer as a healthy, icy snack.

18. Pumpkin and Oatmeal Balls

Ingredients:

- 1 cup canned pumpkin

- 1/2 cup rolled oats

- A sprinkle of ground cinnamon

Process:

1. Mix canned pumpkin, rolled oats, and a sprinkle of ground cinnamon until well combined.

2. Roll into small balls and refrigerate until firm.

19. Broccoli and Cheese Stuffed Toys

Ingredients:

- Hollow dog toys (e.g., Kongs)

- Steamed and chopped broccoli

- Low-fat cheese cubes

Process:

1. Stuff the hollow dog toys with a mixture of steamed and chopped broccoli and low-fat cheese cubes.

2. Seal the opening with a bit of peanut butter.

3. Give the stuffed toys to your dog for a fun and tasty challenge.

20. Carrot and Cucumber Sticks

Ingredients:

- Baby carrots

- Cucumber sticks

Process:

1. Simply offer baby carrots and cucumber sticks as crunchy, low-calorie snacks.

These meat-free, non-baked treats provide a variety of flavors and textures for your dog to enjoy while being nutritious and easy to prepare. Have fun making these homemade goodies for your furry companion!

CAKE TREATS

1. Peanut Butter Banana Cake

Ingredients:

- 1 ripe banana

- 1/4 cup natural peanut butter

- 1 egg

- 1 cup whole wheat flour

- 1 teaspoon baking powder

Process:

1. Preheat your oven to 350°F (175°C) and grease a small cake pan.

2. Mash the ripe banana and mix it with peanut butter and the egg.

3. Gradually add in the whole wheat flour and baking powder, stirring until well combined.

4. Pour the batter into the cake pan.

5. Bake for 20-25 minutes or until a toothpick comes out clean. Allow it to cool before serving.

2. Apple Carrot Cake

Ingredients:

- 1 cup grated apple

- 1/2 cup grated carrot

- 1/4 cup unsweetened applesauce

- 1 egg

- 1 cup whole wheat flour

- 1 teaspoon baking soda

Process:

1. Preheat your oven to 350°F (175°C) and grease a small cake pan.

2. Mix grated apple, grated carrot, unsweetened applesauce, and the egg.

3. Gradually add in the whole wheat flour and baking soda, stirring until well combined.

4. Pour the batter into the cake pan.

5. Bake for 20-25 minutes or until a toothpick comes out clean. Allow it to cool before serving.

3. Pumpkin Spice Cake

Ingredients:

- 1 cup canned pumpkin

- 1/4 cup unsweetened applesauce

- 1/4 cup honey

- 1 egg

- 1 1/2 cups oat flour

- 1/2 teaspoon ground cinnamon

Process:

1. Preheat your oven to 350°F (175°C) and grease a small cake pan.

2. Combine canned pumpkin, unsweetened applesauce, honey, and the egg.

3. Gradually add oat flour and ground cinnamon, stirring until well mixed.

4. Pour the batter into the cake pan.

5. Bake for 25-30 minutes or until a toothpick comes out clean. Allow it to cool before serving.

4. Blueberry Delight Cake

Ingredients:

- 1 cup blueberries

- 1/4 cup plain yogurt

- 1/4 cup honey

- 1 egg

- 1 1/2 cups whole wheat flour

- 1 teaspoon baking powder

Process:

1. Preheat your oven to 350°F (175°C) and grease a small cake pan.

2. Mix blueberries, plain yogurt, honey, and the egg.

3. Gradually add whole wheat flour and baking powder, stirring until well combined.

4. Pour the batter into the cake pan.

5. Bake for 20-25 minutes or until a toothpick comes out clean. Allow it to cool before serving.

5. Carob Cake with Carob Frosting

Ingredients:

- 1 cup carob chips

- 1/4 cup unsweetened applesauce

- 1/4 cup plain yogurt

- 1 egg

- 1 1/2 cups whole wheat flour

- 1 teaspoon baking soda

Process:

1. Preheat your oven to 350°F (175°C) and grease a small cake pan.

2. Melt carob chips and mix them with unsweetened applesauce, plain yogurt, and the egg.

3. Gradually add whole wheat flour and baking soda, stirring until well combined.

4. Pour the batter into the cake pan.

5. Bake for 20-25 minutes or until a toothpick comes out clean.

6. Allow the cake to cool and frost with melted carob chips if desired.

6. Cheesy Veggie Cake

Ingredients:

- 1 cup grated zucchini

- 1/2 cup grated carrot

- 1/2 cup shredded cheddar cheese

- 1 cup whole wheat flour

- 1 teaspoon baking powder

Process:

1. Preheat your oven to 350°F (175°C) and grease a small cake pan.

2. Mix grated zucchini, grated carrot, shredded cheddar cheese, and the egg.

3. Gradually add whole wheat flour and baking powder, stirring until well mixed.

4. Pour the batter into the cake pan.

5. Bake for 20-25 minutes or until a toothpick comes out clean. Allow it to cool before serving.

7. Coconut and Berry Cake

Ingredients:

- 1/2 cup shredded coconut

- 1/4 cup mixed berries (blueberries, strawberries, raspberries)

- 1/4 cup unsweetened applesauce

- 1 egg

- 1 cup oat flour

- 1/2 teaspoon baking powder

Process:

1. Preheat your oven to 350°F (175°C) and grease a small cake pan.

2. Combine shredded coconut, mixed berries, unsweetened applesauce, and the egg.

3. Gradually add oat flour and baking powder, stirring until well combined.

4. Pour the batter into the cake pan.

5. Bake for 20-25 minutes or until a toothpick comes out clean. Allow it to cool before serving.

8. Peanut Butter and Blueberry Cake

Ingredients:

- 1/2 cup natural peanut butter

- 1 cup blueberries

- 1 egg

- 1 1/2 cups oat flour

- 1/2 teaspoon baking soda

Process:

1. Preheat your oven to 350°F (175°C) and grease a small cake pan.

2. Mix natural peanut butter, blueberries, and the egg.

3. Gradually add oat flour and baking soda, stirring until well combined.

4. Pour the batter into the cake pan.

5. Bake for 20-25 minutes or until a toothpick comes out clean. Allow it to cool before serving.

9. Apple and Cheddar Cake

Ingredients:

- 1 cup grated apple

- 1/2 cup shredded cheddar cheese

- 1/4 cup unsweetened applesauce

- 1 egg

- 1 1/2 cups whole wheat flour

- 1/2 teaspoon baking powder

Process:

1. Preheat your oven to 350°F (175°C) and grease a small cake pan.

2. Combine grated apple, shredded cheddar cheese, unsweetened applesauce, and the egg.

3. Gradually add whole wheat flour and baking powder, stirring until well mixed.

4. Pour the batter into the cake pan.

5. Bake for 20-25 minutes or until a toothpick comes out clean. Allow it to cool before serving.

10. Carrot and Pumpkin Cake

Ingredients:

- 1 cup grated carrot

- 1/2 cup canned pumpkin

- 1/4 cup unsweetened applesauce

- 1 egg

- 1 1/2 cups oat flour

- 1/2 teaspoon cinnamon

Process:

1. Preheat your oven to 350°F (175°C) and grease a small cake pan.

2. Mix grated carrot, canned pumpkin, unsweetened applesauce, and the egg.

3. Gradually add oat flour and cinnamon, stirring until well combined.

4. Pour the batter into the cake pan.

5. Bake for 20-25 minutes or until a toothpick comes out clean. Allow it to cool before serving.

11. Banana and Coconut Cake

Ingredients:

- 2 ripe bananas

- 1/2 cup unsweetened shredded coconut

- 1/4 cup plain yogurt

- 1 egg

- 1 1/2 cups whole wheat flour

- 1/2 teaspoon baking soda

Process:

1. Preheat your oven to 350°F (175°C) and grease a small cake pan.

2. Mash the ripe bananas and mix them with shredded coconut, plain yogurt, and the egg.

3. Gradually add whole wheat flour and baking soda, stirring until well mixed.

4. Pour the batter into the cake pan.

5. Bake for 20-25 minutes or until a toothpick comes out clean. Allow it to cool before serving.

12. Berry Bliss Cake

Ingredients:

- 1/2 cup mixed berries (blueberries, strawberries, raspberries)

- 1/4 cup plain yogurt

- 1/4 cup honey

- 1 egg

- 1 1/2 cups oat flour

- 1/2 teaspoon baking powder

Process:

1. Preheat your oven to 350°F (175°C) and grease a small cake pan.

2. Blend mixed berries, plain yogurt, honey, and the egg.

3. Gradually add oat flour and baking powder, stirring until well combined.

4. Pour the batter into the cake pan.

5. Bake for 20-25 minutes or until a toothpick comes out clean. Allow it to cool before serving.

13. Pumpkin and Cranberry Cake

Ingredients:

- 1/2 cup canned pumpkin

- 1/4 cup dried cranberries

- 1/4 cup unsweetened applesauce

- 1 egg

- 1 1/2 cups oat flour

- 1/2 teaspoon nutmeg

Process:

1. Preheat your oven to 350°F (175°C) and grease a small cake pan.

2. Mix canned pumpkin, dried cranberries, unsweetened applesauce, and the egg.

3. Gradually add oat flour and nutmeg, stirring until well combined.

4. Pour the batter into the cake pan.

5. Bake for 20-25 minutes or until a toothpick comes out clean. Allow it to cool before serving.

14. Spinach and Cheese Cake

Ingredients:

- 1 cup chopped spinach

- 1/2 cup shredded cheddar cheese

- 1/4 cup plain yogurt

- 1 egg

- 1 1/2 cups whole wheat flour

- 1/2 teaspoon garlic powder (optional)

Process:

1. Preheat your oven to 350°F (175°C) and grease a small cake pan.

2. Combine chopped spinach, shredded cheddar cheese, plain yogurt, and the egg.

3. Gradually add whole wheat flour and garlic powder (if using), stirring until well mixed.

4. Pour the batter into the cake pan.

5. Bake for 20-25 minutes or until a toothpick comes out clean. Allow it to cool before serving.

15. Coconut and Banana Pupcakes

Ingredients:

- 1 ripe banana

- 1/4 cup unsweetened shredded coconut

- 1/4 cup plain yogurt

- 1 egg

- 1 cup oat flour

- 1/2 teaspoon vanilla extract

Process:

1. Preheat your oven to 350°F (175°C) and prepare cupcake liners in a muffin tin.

2. Mash the ripe banana and mix it with shredded coconut, plain yogurt, egg, and vanilla extract.

3. Gradually add oat flour, stirring until well combined.

4. Divide the batter among cupcake liners.

5. Bake for 15-20 minutes or until a toothpick comes out clean. Allow them to cool before serving.

16. Pumpkin and Zucchini Cake

Ingredients:

- 1/2 cup canned pumpkin

- 1/2 cup grated zucchini

- 1/4 cup unsweetened applesauce

- 1 egg

- 1 1/2 cups oat flour

- 1/2 teaspoon ground ginger

Process:

1. Preheat your oven to 350°F (175°C) and grease a small cake pan.

2. Combine canned pumpkin, grated zucchini, unsweetened applesauce, and the egg.

3. Gradually add oat flour and ground ginger, stirring until well mixed.

4. Pour the batter into the cake pan.

5. Bake for 20-25 minutes or until a toothpick comes out clean. Allow it to cool before serving.

17. Mixed Vegetable Cake

Ingredients:

- 1/2 cup mixed vegetables (peas, carrots, green beans), steamed and chopped

- 1/4 cup unsweetened applesauce

- 1/4 cup plain yogurt

- 1 egg

- 1 1/2 cups whole wheat flour

- 1/2 teaspoon dried parsley (optional)

Process:

1. Preheat your oven to 350°F (175°C) and grease a small cake pan.

2.Combine the steamed and chopped mixed vegetables, unsweetened applesauce, plain yogurt, and the egg.

3. Gradually add the whole wheat flour and dried parsley (if using), stirring until well combined.

4. Pour the batter into the cake pan.

5. Bake for 20-25 minutes or until a toothpick comes out clean. Allow it to cool before serving.

These homemade cake treats offer a variety of flavors and textures for your dog to enjoy while being easy to make and packed with wholesome ingredients. Celebrate special occasions or simply treat your furry friend with these delightful homemade goodies!

LOW-FAT TREATS

1. Pumpkin Biscuits

Ingredients:

- 1 cup canned pumpkin (not pumpkin pie filling)

- 2 cups whole wheat flour

Process:

1. Preheat your oven to 350°F (175°C).

2. Mix canned pumpkin and whole wheat flour until a dough forms.

3. Roll out the dough and cut into desired shapes.

4. Place the biscuits on a baking sheet lined with parchment paper.

5. Bake for 25-30 minutes or until they become firm and lightly browned.

2. Sweet Potato Chewies

Ingredients:

- 2 sweet potatoes

Process:

1. Preheat your oven to 250°F (120°C).

2. Slice sweet potatoes into thin rounds.

3. Place them on a baking sheet lined with parchment paper.

4. Bake for 2-3 hours or until they become chewy.

3. Banana Oat Bites

Ingredients:

- 2 ripe bananas

- 1 cup rolled oats

Process:

1. Preheat your oven to 350°F (175°C).

2. Mash the ripe bananas and mix them with rolled oats.

3. Drop spoonfuls onto a baking sheet lined with parchment paper.

4. Bake for 15-20 minutes or until they become firm.

4. Carrot and Apple Cookies

Ingredients:

- 1 cup grated carrots

- 1 cup grated apple

- 1 1/2 cups oat flour

Process:

1. Preheat your oven to 350°F (175°C).

2. Combine grated carrots, grated apple, and oat flour until a dough forms.

3. Roll out the dough and cut into cookie shapes.

4. Place the cookies on a baking sheet lined with parchment paper.

5. Bake for 15-20 minutes or until they become golden brown.

5. Green Bean Crunchers

Ingredients:

- Fresh green beans

Process:

1. Steam or blanch fresh green beans until they are tender but still crisp.

2. Allow them to cool and serve as a crunchy, low-fat snack.

6. Rice Cake Delights

Ingredients:

- Low-sodium rice cakes

- Natural peanut butter

Process:

1. Spread a thin layer of natural peanut butter on rice cakes.

2. Break the rice cakes into smaller pieces for bite-sized treats.

7. Cucumber Slices

Ingredients:

- Fresh cucumber

Process:

1. Slice fresh cucumber into thin rounds.

2. Offer as a hydrating, low-fat snack.

8. Watermelon Cubes

Ingredients:

- Fresh watermelon, seedless

Process:

1. Cut seedless watermelon into small cubes.

2. Offer as a refreshing, low-calorie treat.

9. Air-Popped Popcorn

Ingredients:

- Plain air-popped popcorn

Process:

1. Pop plain popcorn without added butter or salt.

2. Allow it to cool and offer as a light, low-fat snack.

10. Zucchini Sticks

Ingredients:

- Fresh zucchini

Process:

1. Slice fresh zucchini into thin sticks.

2. Offer as a crisp and low-fat treat.

11. Carrot and Broccoli Biscuits

Ingredients:

- 1 cup grated carrots

- 1/2 cup finely chopped broccoli

- 1 1/2 cups oat flour

Process:

1. Preheat your oven to 350°F (175°C).

2. Combine grated carrots, chopped broccoli, and oat flour until a dough forms.

3. Roll out the dough and cut into biscuit shapes.

4. Place the biscuits on a baking sheet lined with parchment paper.

5. Bake for 15-20 minutes or until they become golden brown.

12. Blueberry and Rice Cakes

Ingredients:

- Low-sodium rice cakes

- Fresh blueberries

Process:

1. Spread a thin layer of natural yogurt on rice cakes.

2. Top each rice cake with fresh blueberries for a fruity and low-fat treat.

13. Banana and Oatmeal Drops

Ingredients:

- 2 ripe bananas

- 1 cup rolled oats

Process:

1. Preheat your oven to 350°F (175°C).

2. Mash the ripe bananas and mix them with rolled oats.

3. Drop spoonfuls onto a baking sheet lined with parchment paper.

4. Bake for 15-20 minutes or until they become firm.

14. Green Pea Popsicles

Ingredients:

- Cooked and cooled green peas

- Low-sodium vegetable broth

Process:

1. Blend cooked and cooled green peas with a bit of low-sodium vegetable broth.

2. Pour the mixture into popsicle molds.

3. Freeze until solid and offer as a refreshing, low-fat popsicle.

15. Spinach and Blueberry Smoothie Cubes

Ingredients:

- Handful of fresh spinach leaves

- Handful of fresh blueberries

- Water

Process:

1. Blend fresh spinach leaves, fresh blueberries, and a little water until smooth.

2. Pour the mixture into ice cube trays.

3. Freeze until solid and serve as a nutrient-packed, low-fat snack.

16. Pumpkin and Zucchini Bites

Ingredients:

- 1/2 cup canned pumpkin

- 1/2 cup grated zucchini

- 1 cup oat flour

Process:

1. Preheat your oven to 350°F (175°C).

2. Mix canned pumpkin, grated zucchini, and oat flour until a dough forms.

3. Shape into small bite-sized balls.

4. Bake for 15-20 minutes or until they become firm.

17. Celery and Carrot Sticks

Ingredients:

- Fresh celery sticks

- Fresh carrot sticks

Process:

1. Simply offer fresh celery and carrot sticks as crunchy, low-fat snacks.

18. Watermelon Ice Cubes

Ingredients:

- Fresh seedless watermelon

Process:

1. Puree fresh seedless watermelon in a blender.

2. Pour the mixture into ice cube trays.

3. Freeze until solid and offer as a hydrating and low-calorie treat.

19. Mixed Berry Gelatin Treats

Ingredients:

- Sugar-free gelatin

- Mixed berries (blueberries, strawberries, raspberries)

Process:

1. Prepare sugar-free gelatin according to the package instructions.

2. Stir in mixed berries.

3. Pour the mixture into silicone molds.

4. Refrigerate until set and serve as a low-fat fruity treat.

20. Banana and Cucumber Slices

Ingredients:

- Fresh banana slices

- Fresh cucumber slices

Process:

1. Offer fresh banana and cucumber slices as a cool and low-fat snack.

These low-fat homemade treats provide a range of flavors and textures for your dog to enjoy while being mindful of their dietary needs. Enjoy making these healthy goodies for your furry companion!

SNACK TREATS

1. Chicken and Rice Bites

Ingredients:

- 1 cup cooked chicken, shredded

- 1 cup cooked rice

- 1/4 cup plain yogurt

Process:

1. Mix cooked and shredded chicken with cooked rice and plain yogurt until well combined.

2. Roll into small bite-sized balls.

3. Refrigerate until they are firm and serve as protein-packed snacks.

2. Sweet Potato and Cinnamon Chips

Ingredients:

- 2 sweet potatoes

- 1 teaspoon ground cinnamon

Process:

1. Preheat your oven to 250°F (120°C).

2. Slice sweet potatoes into thin rounds.

3. Sprinkle with ground cinnamon.

4. Place them on a baking sheet and bake for 2-3 hours until they become crispy.

3. Tuna and Cheddar Biscuits

Ingredients:

- 1 can tuna in water, drained and flaked

- 1/2 cup shredded cheddar cheese

- 1 cup oat flour

Process:

1. Preheat your oven to 350°F (175°C).

2. Mix flaked tuna, shredded cheddar cheese, and oat flour until a dough forms.

3. Roll out the dough and cut into biscuit shapes.

4. Place the biscuits on a baking sheet lined with parchment paper.

5. Bake for 15-20 minutes or until they become golden brown.

4. Peanut Butter and Pumpkin Balls

Ingredients:

- 1/2 cup natural peanut butter

- 1/2 cup canned pumpkin (not pumpkin pie filling)

- 1 cup oatmeal

Process:

1. Mix natural peanut butter, canned pumpkin, and oatmeal until well combined.

2. Form the mixture into small balls.

3. Refrigerate until they are firm and serve as a flavorful snack.

5. Beef and Carrot Jerky

Ingredients:

- Lean beef slices

- Carrot, cut into thin strips

Process:

1. Preheat your oven to the lowest temperature (usually around 170°F or 75°C).

2. Lay lean beef slices and carrot strips on a baking sheet.

3. Bake for several hours (4-6 hours) until they become dry and jerky-like.

6. Salmon and Sweet Potato Treats

Ingredients:

- 1 cup canned salmon, undrained

- 1 cup mashed sweet potato

- 2 cups whole wheat flour

Process:

1. Preheat your oven to 350°F (175°C).

2. Combine canned salmon (with liquid), mashed sweet potato, and whole wheat flour until a dough forms.

3. Roll out the dough and cut into treat shapes.

4. Place the treats on a baking sheet lined with parchment paper.

5. Bake for 20-25 minutes or until they become firm and lightly browned.

7. Turkey and Cranberry Balls

Ingredients:

- 1 cup cooked and ground turkey

- 1/4 cup dried cranberries

- 1/2 cup oat flour

Process:

1. Mix cooked and ground turkey, dried cranberries, and oat flour until well combined.

2. Roll into small bite-sized balls.

3. Refrigerate until they are firm and serve as a savory snack.

8. Spinach and Cheese Squares

Ingredients:

- 1/2 cup chopped spinach

- 1 cup shredded low-fat cheese

- 1 cup oat flour

- 1/4 cup water

Process:

1. Preheat your oven to 350°F (175°C).

2. Combine chopped spinach, shredded cheese, oat flour, and water in a bowl.

3. Press the mixture into a baking dish and flatten it.

4. Bake for 15-20 minutes or until it becomes firm and lightly browned.

5. Cut into squares after cooling.

9. Banana and Blueberry Muffins

Ingredients:

- 2 ripe bananas, mashed

- 1/2 cup fresh blueberries

- 1/4 cup unsweetened applesauce

- 1 cup whole wheat flour

Process:

1. Preheat your oven to 350°F (175°C).

2. Mix mashed bananas, fresh blueberries, unsweetened applesauce, and whole wheat flour until combined.

3. Pour the batter into mini muffin tins.

4. Bake for 15-20 minutes or until a toothpick comes out clean.

10. Veggie Mix Medley

Ingredients:

- Steamed and chopped mixed vegetables (e.g., broccoli, carrots, green beans)

Process:

1. Steam and chop mixed vegetables until they are tender.

2. Allow them to cool and serve as a healthy medley of veggie snacks.

11. Turkey and Sweet Potato Slices

Ingredients:

- Lean turkey slices

- Sweet potato, thinly sliced

Process:

1. Preheat your oven to the lowest temperature (usually around 170°F or 75°C).

2. Lay lean turkey slices and sweet potato slices on a baking sheet.

3. Bake for several hours (4-6 hours) until they become dry and chewy.

12. Carrot and Oatmeal Cookies

Ingredients:

- 1 cup grated carrots

- 1 cup oat flour

- 1/4 cup unsweetened applesauce

Process:

1. Preheat your oven to 350°F (175°C).

2. Mix grated carrots, oat flour, and unsweetened applesauce until a dough forms.

3. Roll out the dough and cut into cookie shapes.

4. Place the cookies on a baking sheet lined with parchment paper.

5. Bake for 15-20 minutes or until they become golden brown.

13. Chicken and Spinach Jerky

Ingredients:

- Boneless, skinless chicken breasts

- Fresh spinach leaves

Process:

1. Preheat your oven to the lowest temperature (usually around 170°F or 75°C).

2. Slice boneless, skinless chicken breasts into thin strips.

3. Lay chicken strips and fresh spinach leaves on a baking sheet.

4. Bake for several hours (3-4 hours) until they become dry and jerky-like.

14. Blueberry and Cottage Cheese Drops

Ingredients:

- 1/2 cup fresh blueberries

- 1/4 cup low-fat cottage cheese

- 1 cup oat flour

Process:

1. Preheat your oven to 350°F (175°C).

2. Blend fresh blueberries and low-fat cottage cheese until smooth.

3. Mix the blueberry-cottage cheese blend with oat flour until a dough forms.

4. Drop spoonfuls onto a baking sheet lined with parchment paper.

5. Bake for 15-20 minutes or until they become firm.

15. Peanut Butter and Carrot Stacks

Ingredients:

- Natural peanut butter

- Sliced carrots

Process:

1. Spread a small amount of natural peanut butter between slices of carrots to create "sandwich" stacks.

2. Serve as a crunchy and satisfying snack.

16. Apple and Cheddar Popsicles

Ingredients:

- Unsweetened applesauce

- Small cubes of cheddar cheese

- Apple slices

Process:

1. Fill ice cube trays with unsweetened applesauce.

2. Place small cubes of cheddar cheese and apple slices into each cube.

3. Freeze until solid and offer as a refreshing treat.

17. Turkey and Veggie Meatballs

Ingredients:

- Lean ground turkey

- Steamed and finely chopped mixed vegetables (e.g., peas, carrots, green beans)

- Cooked brown rice

Process:

1. Combine lean ground turkey, steamed and finely chopped mixed vegetables, and cooked brown rice.

2. Form the mixture into meatballs and bake until cooked through.

3. Allow them to cool before serving.

18. Zucchini and Oat Bites

Ingredients:

- 1 cup grated zucchini

- 1 cup oat flour

- 1/4 cup plain yogurt

Process:

1. Preheat your oven to 350°F (175°C).

2. Mix grated zucchini, oat flour, and plain yogurt until a dough forms.

3. Roll into small bite-sized balls.

4. Refrigerate until they are firm and serve as a light and healthy snack.

19. Turkey and Green Bean Crunchers

Ingredients:

- Cooked and shredded turkey

- Cooked and chopped green beans

Process:

1. Mix cooked and shredded turkey with cooked and chopped green beans.

2. Form the mixture into small crunchy treats.

3. Allow them to cool before serving.

20. Beef and Parsley Biscuits

Ingredients:

- Lean ground beef

- Fresh parsley, finely chopped

- Whole wheat flour

Process:

1. Combine lean ground beef, finely chopped fresh parsley, and whole wheat flour until a dough forms.

2. Roll out the dough and cut into biscuit shapes.

3. Place the biscuits on a baking sheet lined with parchment paper.

4. Bake for 15-20 minutes or until they become golden brown.

These homemade snack treats offer a variety of flavors and textures for your dog to enjoy while being easy to make and packed with wholesome ingredients. Treat your furry friend to these delightful snacks!

REMEMBER TO ALWAYS CHECK WITH YOUR VETERINARIAN BEFORE INTRODUCING NEW TREATS INTO YOUR DOG'S DIET, ESPECIALLY IF THEY HAVE ANY DIETARY RESTRICTIONS OR ALLERGIES.

Printed in Great Britain
by Amazon